Contents

In the nest

This **hen** has laid an egg in her **nest**. Inside the egg a chick is growing.

The mother hen may lay several eggs. Then she sits on the eggs to keep them warm.

Breaking the shell

The baby chickens are ready to hatch. The chick inside this egg has **pecked** through the shell.

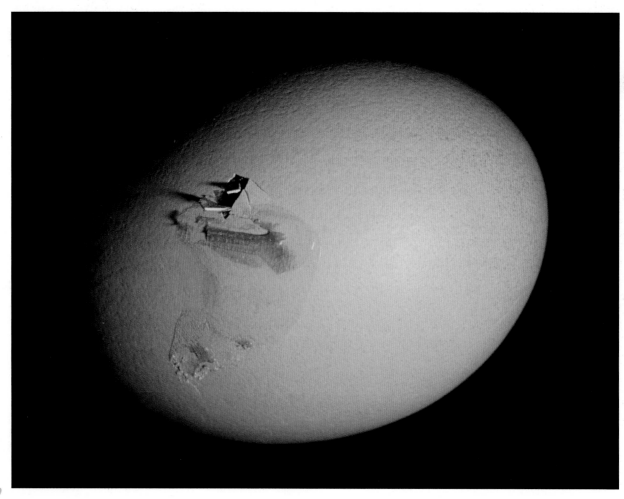

Baby Animals
CHICK

Angela Royston

Chrysalis Children's Books

First published in the UK in 2004 by
Chrysalis Children's Books
An imprint of Chrysalis Books Group Plc
The Chrysalis Building, Bramley Road, London W10 6SP

Paperback edition first published in 2005

ISBN 1 84458 087 3 (hb)
ISBN 1 84458 492 5 (pb)

British Library Cataloguing in Publication Data
for this book is available from the British Library.

Editorial Manager: Joyce Bentley
Editor: Clare Lewis

Produced by Bender Richardson White
Project Editor: Lionel Bender
Designer: Ben White
Production: Kim Richardson
Picture Researcher: Cathy Stastny
Cover Make-up: Mike Pilley, Radius

Printed in China

10 9 8 7 6 5 4 3 2 1

NOTE
In this book, we have used photographs of different types of chicken. Each type has feathers of a certain colour and pattern.

Picture credits
Corbis Images Inc: Robert Pickett 6.
Ecoscene: Sally Morgan 5, 21; Robert Pickett 7, 8; Robin Redfern 16; Angela Hampton 24;
Peter Cairns 28.
Natural History Photo Agency: Henry Ausloos 17.
Oxford Scientific Films: 20, 23, 26.
Rex Features Ltd: Greg Williams 4; Sipa 9; Phanie 19; Organic 22.
RSPCA Photolibrary: E A Janes, cover, 1, 2, 11, 25, 27, 29; Geoff de Feu 10;
Joe B Blossom 12, 13, 15, 18; Angela Hampton 14.

When the hole is big enough, the chick uses its body to push open the shell.

Just hatched

The newly **hatched** chick is wet and very tired. But soon its **feathers** dry.

Not all of the eggs hatch at the same time. This new chick is taking its first look around.

First few hours

Each new chick is covered with soft feathers called **down**. Down keeps the chicks warm.

The mother hen **clucks** softly.
The chicks huddle close to her
to keep warm and safe.

A few days old

The mother hen pecks for **grain** and other food. The chicks copy their mother.

The chicks soon learn to feed themselves. When they are thirsty, they drink some water.

Sleeping

Each mother hen and her chicks live in a nesting box. The hen comes out first each morning.

At night this hen climbs into her box and the chicks creep under her wings for warmth.

One week old

The chicks follow behind their mother. She watches out for foxes and other dangers.

When she is alarmed, she clucks loudly. The chicks run with her to the nesting box.

Two weeks old

New strong feathers are beginning to grow through the chicks' soft down.

The chicks' **claws** grow strong, too. They use them to scratch the ground for food.

Eight weeks old

The chicks are growing bigger. Now they have long feathers instead of down.

Each chick has a red
comb on its head and a
red **wattle** on its neck.

Ten weeks old

The chicks are old enough to leave their mother and live with the other chickens.

They run around and flap their wings, but they cannot fly more than a few metres.

Perching to sleep

In the evening, the hens and chicks go to the hen house, where they sleep at night.

They **perch** on poles above the ground. They cling to the poles with their claws.

Four months

This young hen is cleaning her feathers. She uses her **beak** like a comb.

The hen needs smooth, clean feathers to keep out the rain.

Five months old

The chicks are now fully grown. This young hen begins to lay her own eggs.

A young male chicken is called a **rooster**. He sometimes calls 'cock-a-doodle-doo!'

Quiz

1 What does a chick use to break through its shell?

2 What do hens and chicks most like to eat?

3 Why do hens need to keep their feathers clean?

4 How far can hens fly?

5 What do we call the brightly coloured flaps of skin
a) on a chicken's head b) on a chicken's neck?

6 What sound does a mother hen make as an alarm?

7 How old are chicks when fully grown?

8 What is a young male chicken called?

The answers are all in this book!

New Words

beak hard structure that sticks out from a bird's mouth instead of lips; also called a bill.

claws curved nails on the toes of birds and some other animals.

cluck sound made by a hen.

comb red flap of skin on top of a chicken's head; a toothed instrument for cleaning and straightening hair.

down soft first feathers that keep a baby bird warm.

feather part of a bird's body that covers its skin. Feathers allow the bird to fly and keep water off its body.

grain small seeds, such as wheat, barley and corn.

hatch when a baby bird breaks out of an egg.

hen a female bird, such as a chicken.

nest home of straw or grass made especially for baby animals.

peck when a bird bites with its beak.

perch rest on a pole, branch of a tree or another similar support.

rooster a young male chicken.

wattle red flap of skin on a bird's neck.

Index

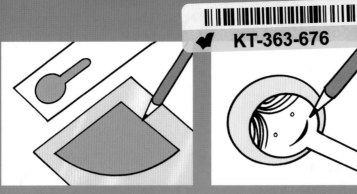

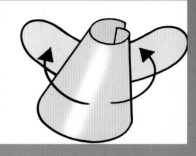

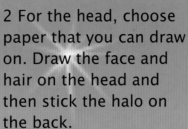

1 Copy the templates on the back cover onto card. Choose one colour for the dress and another for the halo and wings.

2 For the head, choose paper that you can draw on. Draw the face and hair on the head and then stick the halo on the back.

3 Curl the dress piece into a cone, tape in place, and snip off the top. Glue the wings on the back. Finally insert the head.

Add a star cut from card if you wish.

2 Very berry bottles

Berries are a reminder of the harvests that provide the Christmas feast.

   Look out for leftover bottles and jars in interesting shapes, to decorate and fill with real berry twigs or ones you make.

1 Choose a jar or bottle that will hold Christmas twigs prettily. Paint it all over with gesso. Let it dry, then paint again.

2 Collect twigs and put them in your bottle.

3 Make bright berries by looping red beads on florist's wire. Add them to the decoration.

3 A card to keep

This greetings card is sized to be a perfect bookmark – so it's a card and a gift in one.

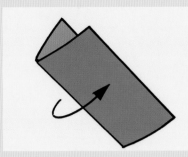

1 Cut a piece of card 20cm x 10cm. Fold in half lengthways.

2 Cut a tree shape: a triangle nearly 19cm tall and nearly 5cm wide. Mark where you want "decorations" and punch holes.

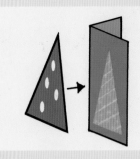

3 Cut a piece of wrapping paper a bit smaller than the tree. Stick this on the card, then the tree on top. Add a star at the top.

4 Brilliant bags

It's quite easy to learn how to wrap a box neatly… but not all presents come in boxes. This page shows you how to use the box method to make a bag.

You will need to find a leftover box such as a cereal packet or shoebox to help you make your bag.

Add a decoration – such as a star or the bows from page 5.

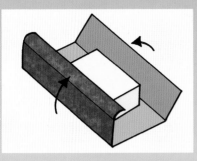

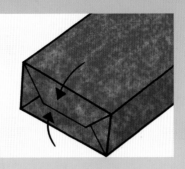

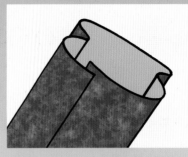

1 Take a large rectangle of paper to go around your box and tape the join. Leave enough sticking out at the lower end for the base.

2 Now squash the short sides of the paper into the base and crease. Then fold the lower flap up and the top flap down and tape.

3 Crease the long edges of the paper along the empty box then lift the box out. Put the gift in the bag, pleat the narrow sides in from the creased edges, and then fold the top down. Tape shut.

5 Take a bow

Wrapping paper can be expensive. Use small strips of fabulous Christmas paper to brighten up a more thriftily wrapped package.

Have fun practising with any sort of scrap paper. The sizes given here are a good start.

1 Cut three strips of paper 20cm x 1.5cm. Mark the centre point of each and glue one on top of another like this.

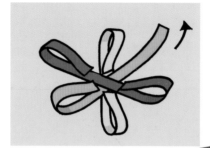

2 Fold the ends to the centre and glue or staple.

3 Add a sticker to the centre. Glue your bow to your package.

Once you have the hang of making paper bows as in step 1, try arranging them crosswise or petal-wise. Use double-sided tape to stack the bows and add a centre topping.

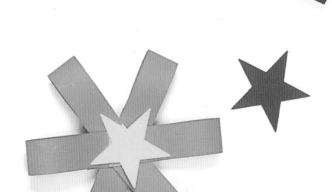

For a double bow, make a small one to fit on top of a big one.

6 Fantastic folds

Jazz up your Christmas tree with lots of these paper-fold decorations. The basic shape is super-simple, so you can have fun varying the extras.

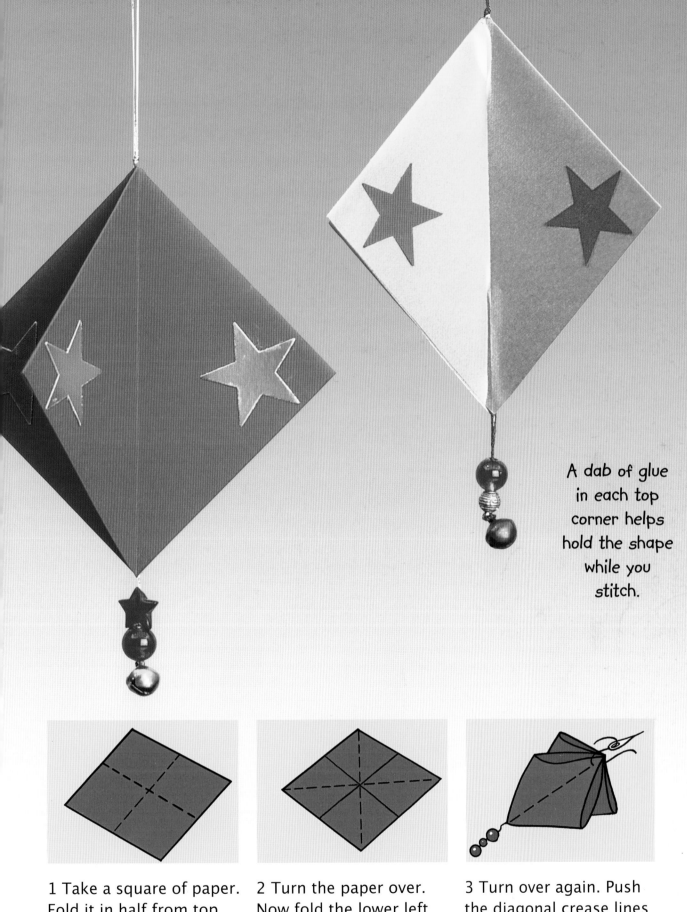

A dab of glue in each top corner helps hold the shape while you stitch.

1 Take a square of paper. Fold it in half from top to bottom, crease, and unfold. Then fold side to side, crease, and unfold.

2 Turn the paper over. Now fold the lower left corner to the top right corner, crease, and unfold. Then fold the lower right corner to the top left corner, crease, and unfold.

3 Turn over again. Push the diagonal crease lines up to give the shape shown. Use a needle and thread to add a hanging loop at the top and a string of beads at the bottom.

7 Surprise gifts

This is a simple way to wrap gifts in a cracker shape. Put a tiny gift or sweet in each one, and place one at every table setting at the Christmas feast.

If a grown-up approves, you could tape a proper cracker snap strip to the tube before you wrap it, so your crackers will pop when you pull them.

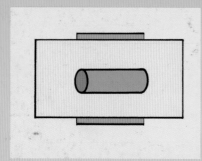  

1 Choose a cardboard tube in which the gift will fit. Cut a rectangle of paper two and a bit times as long as the tube and wide enough to go round it and about 1cm more! Also cut a piece that is as long as the tube and big enough to wrap it with 2cm overlap.

2 With the paper wrong side up and long edge towards you, measure and mark the mid point. Fold the sides to the middle and crease. Rule a line 2cm away from each of the creases as shown. Snip wedge shapes from the crease to the line.

3 Unfold the paper and roll it right side out round the tube. Tie as shown with curling ribbon. Wrap the smaller piece of paper round the tube part and tape shut.

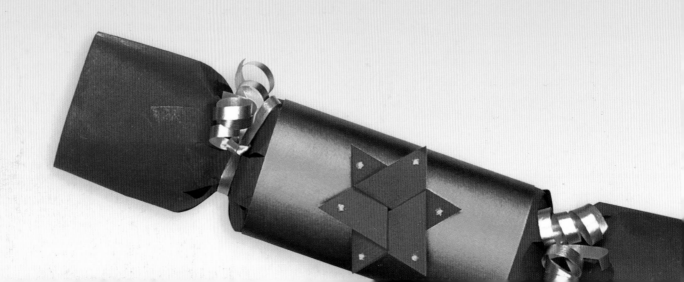

Find out how to make the stars on the next page.

8 Six-point star

In the Christmas story, the wise men followed a star as they brought gifts. What better design for a gift tag!

Use these stars as surprise tags for the gifts you give. They look great on the crackers on the previous page. Make a practice one to get the hang of the folding and writing.

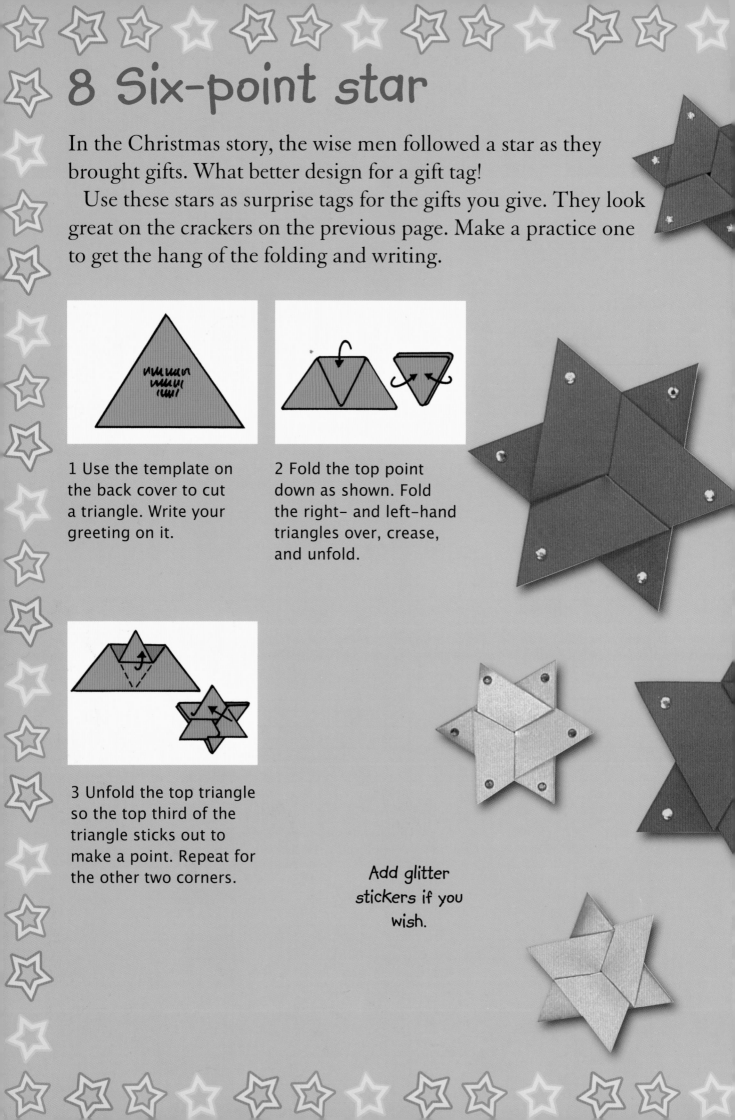

1 Use the template on the back cover to cut a triangle. Write your greeting on it.

2 Fold the top point down as shown. Fold the right- and left-hand triangles over, crease, and unfold.

3 Unfold the top triangle so the top third of the triangle sticks out to make a point. Repeat for the other two corners.

Add glitter stickers if you wish.

9 Simple stockings

Stockings are part of the legend of Santa Claus – a bishop of long ago who gave gifts in secret to a poor family.

These stockings are easy to hang storybook-style to make a festive display. If you don't have a real mantelpiece, you could decorate a piece of dowel or even a straight branch to hang them from. Put the display where the secret gift-giver is bound to find them.

1 Copy the stocking shape here, or draw round a sock you like. Cut two pieces this shape from felt. Also cut a cuff to go round the top of both with a little extra.

2 Place the main pieces like this. Then thread a needle with bright yarn, knot one end, and use an in-and-out stitch to stitch the cuff to the top of first one side of the stocking and then the other.

3 Fold the cuff so the sides match up and stitch around the sides, leaving the top open. Fasten off with a couple of stitches on top of each other.

To hang these, use a needle to thread a piece of strong yarn through the top back corner. Knot the yarn into a hanging loop.

10 Santa's Little Helper

Santa may be the stuff of legends, but you can be a really useful helper around the house at Christmas, and this apron will keep your party clothes clean. The secret gift-giver is bound to be pleased…

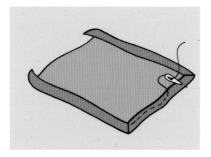

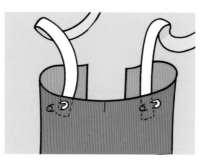

1 Ask a grown-up to help you tear a rectangle of cotton fabric long enough to wrap tightly around you under your armpits and hang to your knees. Pull away the fraying threads, turn 1cm under all round, and stitch.

2 Cut two strips of stout tape, each about 60cm long. Find the centre of the top edge of fabric and measure a point 8cm away either side. Safety-pin the tape in place as shoulder straps at this point.

3 Hold the apron in place as you would wear it and ask a grown-up to safety-pin the right strap to the left back edge and the left strap to the right back edge. Take off the apron and stitch the straps in place.

Add buttons where the straps join the apron at the front.

11 Christmas pudding truffles

You can whizz these truffles together in no time. They are full of dried fruits, like a real Christmas pudding… but with chocolate to hold them together.

Ask a grown-up before you prepare any food, and wash your hands.

You will need:

200g chopped dates
200g raisins
200g ground almonds
60g chocolate, chopped or
    grated

also
ready-to-roll icing in
    white, green, and red

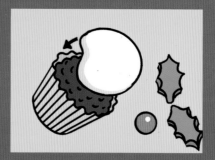

1 Put the dates, raisins, and ground almonds in a blender and whizz to make a squidgy mass. Add the chocolate and whizz a bit more.

2 Put the mass into a bowl and squeeze into a ball. Then pull off small amounts and roll each into a small ball that will fit a truffle case.

3 Roll out the white icing. Cut tiny circles and drape these over each truffle. Roll out the green icing and cut a pair of leaves for each truffle. Then roll tiny balls of red icing and add on top.

12 Pyramid box

You could put any small gift in this box and hang it on the tree.
  The shape of this box makes it an amusing way to give a super-size truffle. Make the base big enough to fit the truffle. Protect each truffle with cellophane or foil before putting inside this card box.

1 Copy the template shape on the back cover and draw round it onto your choice of card. Cut it out.

2 Mark the centre points and rule the crease lines as shown. Use a ruler to help you fold up each side in turn.

3 Punch a hole at the three points. Add your gift. Use ribbon or a chenille wire to hold the gift shut.

13 Snowball cakes

Ask a grown-up before you do any cooking, and wash your hands.
  To bake the cakes, you will need the oven to be heated to 170°C.
Put paper cases into a 12-hole muffin tray.

You will need:

cake
  60g butter at room
    temperature
  200g caster sugar
  180g self-raising flour
  30g desiccated coconut
  2 medium eggs, beaten
  120ml cream or coconut
    milk
icing
  50g butter
  up to 200g icing sugar
  1 tablespoon cream or
    coconut milk
  100g desiccated coconut

1 First the cake: put the butter, sugar, flour, and coconut in a bowl and mix with a hand-held electric mixer until the butter is cut fine. Stir in the eggs and cream together.

2 Put spoonfuls of the mix in each muffin case and bake for 25 minutes. Leave to cool. Meanwhile, put the icing sugar and butter in a bowl and mix with a hand-held mixer until the butter is cut fine. Mix in the cream until you have a fluffy paste.

3 Spread the icing generously on each of the cakes. Tip desiccated coconut onto a shallow bowl and dip each cake in it.

You can add other
decorations if you like.
Try silver balls for a
frosty look.

14 Drinks party

Christmas parties are thirsty affairs. This spicy drink will keep you going.

Ask a grown-up before you do any cooking, and wash your hands.

You will need:

2 small oranges
whole cloves
1 litre apple juice
1 tablespoon honey
2 cinnamon sticks

1 Take the small oranges and stick them with whole cloves. You may need a fork to pierce the skin so the cloves go in easily.

2 Into a saucepan pour the apple juice, and add the oranges, honey, and cinnamon sticks. Heat gently until just simmering and allow to bubble for about 5 minutes.

3 Leave the juice to cool for about 10 minutes. Pour it into a warmed jug and serve in warm mugs or glasses.

It is simple to warm the jugs and mugs by immersing them in a sink of tap-hot water for a few minutes, then draining and drying.

Float thinly cut apple
slices in each glass
for a stylish look.

15 Note of thanks

Part of Christmas is giving. Another part is saying thank you.

This simple thank-you note can be made from a square of used wrapping paper. You might even be able to use a scrap of ribbon to finish it prettily.

 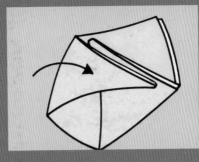 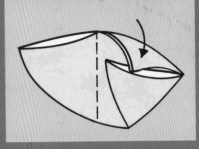

1 Cut a square of paper, about 20cm x 20cm. If you want to line your note, cut or tear another square slightly smaller and glue it on the wrong side of the first piece. Write your note.

2 Fold the square note-side in like this: bottom corner to top and crease. Right point to mid-left side and left point to mid-right side. Crease.

3 Unfold just the left point and fold down the top points, then tuck them in between the layers of the right-hand fold. Refold the left point, punch a hole, and tie through all layers.

Don't fret about how to say thanks. Just the words "Thank You" (and your name) beautifully written and prettily presented will be much appreciated.

16 Peppermint creams

These sweets are quick to make and fun to decorate.
Ask a grown-up before you do any cooking, and wash your hands.

300g icing sugar
2 tablespoons cream
1 egg white, lightly
   whisked
peppermint essence
200g chocolate
   sprinkles

1 Sieve the icing sugar into a bowl. Stir in the egg white and peppermint essence. Add the cream drop by drop till you have a stiff paste.

2 Roll the paste into a sausage shape. Slice into discs about 1cm thick. Put on cake cases and leave to dry.

3 When you are ready, break the chocolate into a bowl and ask a grown-up to melt it in a microwave. Dip each peppermint cream in the chocolate. Add decorations before the chocolate sets.